Clean Eating: A Guide to Health and Wellness

Clean Eating Recipes for the Entire Family

By: Amy Zulpa

Table of Contents

Publishers Notes 3

Dedication 4

Chapter 1- Clean Eating- What Does It All Mean 5

Chapter 2- The Intrinsic Benefits of Clean Eating 10

Chapter 3- How to Get the Hormones and Chemicals Out Of the Diet 15

Chapter 4- How to Maintain the Clean Diet When Dining Out 21

Chapter 5- 10 Clean Eating Breakfast Recipes 26

Chapter 6- 10 Clean Eating Soup & Salad Recipes 34

Chapter 7- 10 Clean Eating Main Course Recipes 42

About the Author 50

Publishers Notes

Disclaimer

This publication is intended to provide helpful and informative material. It is not intended to diagnose, treat, cure, or prevent any health problem or condition, nor is intended to replace the advice of a physician. No action should be taken solely on the contents of this book. Always consult your physician or qualified health-care professional on any matters regarding your health and before adopting any suggestions in this book or drawing inferences from it.

The author and publisher specifically disclaim all responsibility for any liability, loss or risk, personal or otherwise, which is incurred as a consequence, directly or indirectly, from the use or application of any contents of this book.

Any and all product names referenced within this book are the trademarks of their respective owners. None of these owners have sponsored, authorized, endorsed, or approved this book.

Always read all information provided by the manufacturers' product labels before using their products. The author and publisher are not responsible for claims made by manufacturers.

© 2013

Manufactured in the United States of America

DEDICATION

This book is dedicated to my family.

Chapter 1- Clean Eating- What Does It All Mean

Clean eating has become a movement, being mentioned everywhere! It may sound easy but what really is clean eating? It is not a diet and it is not a plan with strict uneasy rules. Unlike counting calories, clean eating does not require counting, subtracting, or any types of calculations. So, get that out of your head! No more starving to lose weight or get healthy. Simply, eat pure and clean food. How do you do this? Follow the steps below and you will be on your way to a much healthier and happier lifestyle.

There is actually a variety of perspectives when it comes to clean eating. Because of this, many people have a lot of questions and concerns when they decide to do this. There is no need to over think things! Clean eating is very simple.

Clean eating is all about eating foods that are in its most natural state. There are some things you need to stay away from. These include: processed foods, foods with a high amount of preservatives, foods with tons of sugar in it, and foods with unhealthy fats. Unhealthy fats are any saturated or trans fats. Avoid these at all costs! To get down to it, these types of foods have either had all of their nutrition taken away or been injected with chemicals.

Unlike diets, clean eating does not have a handbook with exact rules on what to do. I will share my interpretation on what to do. Eat three full meals and two small snacks per day.

What to eat:

1. Whole grains
2. Fresh local fruits and vegetables, preferably organic
3. Free range and grass fed meats/fish
4. Dairy
5. More vegetables than meat per week
6. A LOT of water or diet drinks but NOT diet soda
7. Healthy fats: nuts, avocados, organic coconut oils, etc.
8. Soy
9. Tofu

A major point that I want to get across is to make healthy cooking choices. Instead of eating out, always try to prepare your own food so you are aware of what you are consuming. Even at work or school, take a cooler or lunch bag for lunch. When cooking at home, stick to baking, steaming, or light sautéing.

Make sure to stick to foods that are in its natural state. This is pretty self explanatory; have nothing man-made. For example, you choose to eat broccoli. You cannot add cheese, butter, breadcrumbs, or anything of that nature and then bake it for 45 minutes. This is taking away all of the nutrition! Instead, add a little olive oil, lemon juice, and light fresh Parmesan cheese and then steam it. This is a much better option and it will taste just as amazing!

To address the concerns on clean eating will only benefit the clean eater more. It has everything to do with one's mindset not the body. Many critics believe that if an individual stops eating everything that is unnatural that it will have negative effects on that individual's mind. They think that eating disorders can arise if one is obsessed with only eating clean. To point out, eating clean is not the ONLY thing to do when trying to get healthy or lose weight. Along with eating clean, daily exercise is also very important. When this is done, you will see the positive results much faster.

Learning to eat clean is about simplifying and not overdoing the preparation of the meal. It is much healthier and much easier! No need to get obsessive about it. If you are at a birthday party and cake is being offered, you do not need to turn it down because you are afraid that it is not clean. This is an occasion. You can make up for it by exercising later. Clean eating is not being perfect. It is being consistent MOST of the time. Don't stress over a bowl of pasta once a week. Try to be consistent with eating clean 80% of the time. You will reach your health goals if you abide by that one guideline.

Now on to the expenses: A lot of you are probably thinking you cannot eat clean because organics and free-range meat are too expensive. This is a myth! You can actually buy what you need for less than what you are probably spending on all of the chemical filled food.

You also need to become more familiar with labeling. Natural foods have only 1-2 ingredients in them so if there is a huge list of ingredients, stay away from it. To be clear, fat free and sugar free foods are not considered clean eating. Those foods have been chemically manipulated. These foods are just as unhealthy for you as the high fat and high sugar filled foods.

Last but not least what are some of the health benefits of clean eating? First off, eating clean will help cut down on the risks of the onset of serious health conditions or diseases. Second, the most obvious is weight loss. Clean eating will help your body get back to normal because all those unhealthy fats and chemicals are very abnormal for a human body even though you might be used to them. They are hurting your body at a pretty fast rate. More benefits include: boosting your immune system, being more energized throughout your days, improving your cholesterol levels, balancing out your blood sugar, improving your sleep and mood, and general increases in your overall health.

Clean eating is an excellent decision for everyone. It will allow you to start leading a much healthier and improved life. The way you eat controls a lot of things. So, if you embark on clean eating, who knows what you can accomplish next!

CHAPTER 2- THE INTRINSIC BENEFITS OF CLEAN EATING

Eating a diet that is free of harmful chemicals like preservatives and other hormone-altering substances has several benefits. While it can be a challenge to eat clean, since many of the foods found in supermarkets are heavily processed, the intrinsic advantages of a clean diet can serve both you and your family well. Here are some of the positive results you can expect.

You'll Have More Energy

When you're getting adequate vitamins and nutrients from your body, you'll be more productive throughout the day because your energy levels will be higher. Nutrients like iron and B-vitamins are present in many clean foods, and these substances are essential for helping your cells to gain energy so they can work properly.

Your blood sugar levels are also directly related to your energy, and eating clean helps to keep your blood sugar balanced. A spike in your blood sugar, which almost immediately reduces energy, can occur if you're consuming too many simple carbohydrates like processed baked goods or white rice and pasta. In fact, the Michigan State University Extension suggests eating a breakfast that contains whole grains, which will keep you full until lunch without raising your blood sugar too high.

Your Heart Will Be Healthier

Eating clean helps to make you healthier overall, and a diet that is full of vitamin-rich foods will lower your chances of developing cardiovascular disease. Consuming lots of raw vegetables and fruits supply your body with Vitamin C, which helps to strengthen your blood vessels. Eating these foods regularly decreases the chances of heart disease by promoting healthy circulation and supplying the body with antioxidants that reduce the likelihood of hypertension and stroke.

Consuming healthy fats is also a part of eating clean; consuming nuts, cooking with olive oil and consuming avocado in its natural form lowers LDL or "bad" cholesterol which makes the heart healthier.

Your Mind Will Be Sharper

Eating clean not only provides physical benefits, but can improve the way your mind functions as well. For instance, Vitamin B6, which is found in foods like pistachios, tuna and bananas, assist the body in creating dopamine. Dopamine is created in the brain and assists the body in feeling happiness or pleasure.

Omega-3 fatty acids, which are abundant in foods like salmon, eggs and almonds, are also essential for mental health. If you're not getting enough omega-3s, it is common to feel depressed or moody.

The Norris Cotton Cancer Center also asserts that reducing the amount of caffeine in your diet can make your clean eating efforts more effective. Caffeine has the ability to increase anxiety, which can increase cortisol. Cortisol is commonly referred to as the 'stress hormone,' and can cause weight gain, especially in the stomach area, if too much is created in the body.

It's also important not to skip meals. Eating clean at every meal can help you avoid headaches or mental fogginess and provide your brain with the necessary vitamins and minerals to concentrate on challenging tasks.

You'll Lower Your Risk of Cancer

When you're eating a clean diet, you're helping your body to fight off cancer. When there are lots of processed foods in your diet, there is a greater chance that cancer will develop in your body, according to the Colorado State University Extension. Foods that are fried, as well as those high in saturated fat and processed meats like bologna and hot dogs can all increase cancer risk. A clean diet that consists of lean meats, whole grains and lots of fruits and vegetables increases your phyto-nutrient intake, which combats cancer growth. Colorado State University asserts that raw foods like tomatoes, broccoli and kale are especially beneficial when protecting the body against cancer.

You'll Lose Pounds (& Keep Them Off)

Even if you're following an exercise program, chances are you won't see the changes you want in your body if you're not eating well. Eating food that is free of preservatives and filled with vitamins and minerals will help you to lose weight at a faster rate and make your workouts even more satisfying. Consuming lean meats and whole grains as part of your lifestyle will also help you to keep unwanted pounds from returning.

You'll Enhance Your Immune System

Filling your body with essential vitamins and minerals makes your immune system stronger. This means that free radicals and toxins will not affect your immune system as much, since you'll be able to fight off viruses and impurities at a faster rate. And if you do happen to catch a cold or get the flu as a result of being exposed to others who are sick, eating clean will help you to recover quicker. A stronger immune system also means fewer trips to the doctor, which can save you time and money.

Your Level of Confidence Will Increase

A clean diet will make for a slimmer body and a sharper mind, which will increase your confidence. Once you've made this life change, chances are you'll be more likely to conquer other challenges in your life, such as pursuing a new career or completing a degree. Eating clean will likely inspire your friends and family, who may come to you for pointers and advice after seeing how well this way of life, is working for you. Your self-assuredness will increase as you continue to be a positive influence on those you care about, while maintaining your own healthy habits.

Chapter 3 - How to Get the Hormones and Chemicals Out of the Diet

So you are looking to improve your health, and you are doing everything within your means and budget to sustain a well-balanced, low-fat diet. Days have become rituals where many persons take multi-vitamin supplements, eat fresh fruits and vegetables, and of course whole-grain and organic foods. However, is this all really enough?

The harsh reality of it is that at least 80% of our food supply contains GMO's, as well as growth hormones, chemicals/preservatives, all of which deteriorate your health if not immediately, over a period of time. Although some people feel safer selecting foods labeled "organic", a deeper look into our food chain has revealed that most store bought food, including meats, milk, fruits and vegetables, are all by-products of genetic engineering or man-made manipulation of some sort.

Toxic chemicals, including some levels of radiation have also been reported to be present in our food supply, particularly over the last two decades. These reasons may be a result of irradiated water sources, as well as preservatives and pesticides. Food produces make a point to make money and make it fast, even if it's at the expense of the consumer. Why? The truth of the matter is that only we are responsible for researching and paying attention to what we are putting into our bodies.

The manufacturer does not force you to eat or buy its products; they simply bring it to the chains. For this reason, certain level of false advertising may be considered acceptable, as long as there is no blatant terminology used in food labeling. For example, food labeled "all-natural, organic, USDA organic certified," are all misleading terms that can be taken out of context. Unless a product specifically reads "100% organic", you can be sure that the food can contain at least 30% GMO's.

When it comes to growth hormones, you can look for labeling that says "hormone-free, no added hormones or steroids". Regular foods that come with food and nutrition labels usually use scientific names to hide chemicals in food products. Terms such as "Propylene Glycol", a modified algin and chemical that can be found in both foods and a number of consumer products such as toothpaste will alert you to what to eat and what not to.

Although scanning through the labels of products and learning scientific names for these words may be a little inconvenient, it is ultimately your responsibility to avoid these chemical and hormone-filled foods in order to omit them from your diet. Beware of foods that contain no labels (usually the cheapest, and are always on sale), as well as barcode labeling that contains 5 numbers beginning with an 8, as these are all genetically modified and contain various hormones and chemicals.

You may be thinking that the food industry may be making a point to destroy your health, but the fact is food manufacturers want to find alternate ways to produce food in higher quantities at a cheaper price, while selling them for a higher price. Their objective in inducing quicker growth in fruits and vegetables is to sell them all year round, without the delay of waiting for seasonal harvests. They want to place chemical preservatives in the food to sustain their shelf life in order to save more money. They want to inject hormones into the meats in order to make them larger and genetically modify them so that they will grow at a more rapid speed. It's all horrifying, and hard to fathom, but it's the sick sad truth.

So now that you are aware of the tactics of your food manufacturers, seeing that they are not in the health/medical business, but the business of making money. Seeing that they are in the business of making foods taste and look great, regardless of its cost to your well-being, you are probably feeling helpless. If you have no control of the food industry, then obviously you have no other options right? Wrong!

The truth is in spite of what the major food industries and store chains are selling in your grocery aisles, there are choices you can make to greatly lessen, if not totally eliminate chemicals and hormones from your diet. So where do you begin? Remember to only buy products labeled "100% organic", as the FDA is not allowed to label products 100% organic unless they are absolutely that.

Another trick of the trade is to visit your local farmer's market. While it may sound absurd to new-timers, it is actually not all that uncommon. Farmer's markets or local farmers in your area grow their own vegetation on land and raise their own cattle and other livestock. A farmer's market willingly offers supplies of fresh organic fruits and vegetables, and often organic meats too. If you should decide to buy meat from a farmer's market, make sure it's a trusted and inspected one where the meat is refrigerated by the use of a generator, and not sitting out in the sun.

With shopping at your farmer's markets you are encouraging the natural production of organic foods. You are also helping your local community, avoiding third party handlers such as processing plants and labs, and saving a load of money at the same time. Farmer's markets have grown so much over the last few years that many of them are approved for accepting SNAP benefits. It goes to show you how far farmer's markets have evolved!

Another major issue infiltrating our everyday diet with the concern of chemicals and hormones in mind can be found directly in our very own water supply. Although water used to be considered one of the best ways to flush out the body of toxins and waste, over the past few decades bottled water, as well as tap water has been verified to contain the presence of hormones and chemicals.

One major concern is with the hormone Estrogen, which is a more commonly found hormone in our water supply. Typical at home water filtration systems show little success in eliminating these hormones, however studies conducted with a GCB (graphitized carbon black) water filtration system removed a whopping 95.5% of hormones such as Estrogen. Although a little costly, one can buy this filter online, as well as filters designed to remove various chemical build-up such as lead and arsenic, even removing radiation!

If you are looking for something more advanced, and ready to take on a new age technological approaches in removing hormones and chemicals from your diet, a beneficial source would be to purchase a food ozonizer (Ozone Food and water sterilizer). A food ozonizer is the innovative, revolutionary approach of the century. The device has been on the market for a while and proven to remove 80-95% of pesticides, hormones, and antibiotics from meats and vegetables. An addition of fiber supplements or fiber in powder form added to a diet will also kick up the remedy in removing toxins and chemicals from the body and improve overall health.

Chapter 4 - How to Maintain the Clean Diet When Dining Out

Remember that just because you have chosen to maintain a clean diet does not mean that you want to, or should have to, avoid going out to eat. Eating out can be a form of stress relief and a time to bond with friends or family. It gives you an opportunity to relax in an environment other than your home and allows you to try foods that you might not feel like or have the skills to prepare. However, in order to eat out when following clean eating principles you may have to do a little research and get creative with your food choices. Also, keep in mind that eating out may not be an entirely clean experience but there are many things you can do to limit your intake of processed foods at any restaurant.

Do Some Research

Just like you should take a look at your grocery shopping habits when you begin to eat clean you should also take the time to critically assess your habits when dining out. Being prepared before you face a dining situation helps you to make better choices. It also helps you to control which situations you enter. Here are some things to consider:

Do your favorite restaurants have online nutritional information? Many chain restaurants post ingredient lists and nutritional information on their websites. You can use this information to compile a list of acceptable foods before you go out. This saves you time and confusion while ordering. It also helps you figure out if there are certain restaurants you should just cut from your life altogether.

Some restaurants are more substitution-friendly than others. If a restaurant does not allow you to substitute your side-dish for a salad or steamed veggies then perhaps it is time you start looking for a different locale. Make a list of restaurants that are supportive of various diets and suggest them as options when you are going out with a group.

Call ahead. If you are uncomfortable asking a lot of dietary questions in front of your friends then you can call the restaurant ahead of time to discuss what options they have for a clean diet. Larger chains tend to be more responsive to special needs but it never hurts to try contacting small, family operated businesses and asking if they are able to accommodate your dietary choices.

Take Nothing for Granted

Perhaps you assume that chicken or fish is always the most healthy, basic food choice there is at a restaurant. While this may be true some of the time it is certainly not always true. Many times chicken is prepared with many different spices and sauces that do not make it the optimum choice for healthy eating.

Ask your waiter. Don't be afraid to ask your waiter about dishes you want to order. They should be aware of how the food is prepared, or willing to ask the chef for you.

Assume most dishes are over-salted. Restaurants tend to over salt their dishes in order to bring out the most flavors. You can safely order reduced salt or no salt on your dish and then control the amount you add at your table.

Adjust Your Order

You may be the type of person who has always ordered the same menu item from a restaurant for years. When you begin eating clean it is almost certainly time to adjust that order. Small adjustments, such as the following, easily make your dining experience cleaner.

Order Water

Avoid sodas, beers, or juices at restaurants. Water allows you to drink as much as you want, staying as long as you would like, without adding empty calories to your meal.

Avoid Appetizers and Desserts

Most appetizers and desserts are overly processed, often fried, and filled with empty calories. They also tend to make a restaurant meal too large for a single individual. Stick to a single main dish or a few side-orders.

Substitute Sauces and Dressings

You can ask for sauces or dressings on the side. This allows you to control the amount you put on your dish. If you notice your dish comes with a particularly complex sauce you can ask to substitute it altogether for a healthier option.

Order Sides

Sometimes your best option is to make a meal out of sides. Foods like a plain baked potato, steamed vegetables, and a salad may be your cleanest options at a restaurant.

Ask For a Box

Most restaurants tend to serve food in larger portions than necessary. You can easily split a meal between two people and find yourself full and satisfied. Yet many people overeat at restaurants simply because the food is on their plate. When you order your meal ask for a box and immediately put half of your meal in the box to take home and eat later. Some restaurants will happily pack half of your meal, bringing out a smaller portion on your plate.

Eating out is an important part of everyday life. Although some people are happily able to completely cut out restaurant meals others see no need to. Whatever your take on restaurants it is important to realize that it is possible to maintain a clean diet no matter where you are, and easiest to maintain it when you are in the company of friends who maintain the same dietary standards as yourself.

Chapter 5- 10 Clean Eating Breakfast Recipes

Blackberry Apricot French Toast

Ingredients

4 slices whole grain bread, reduced calorie

3 large eggs

2 egg whites

1 tablespoon safflower oil

2 teaspoon orange zest

4 oz frozen blackberries, thawed

4 dried apricot halves, diced

¼ cup water

½ teaspoon pure vanilla extract

2 packets natural sweetener

Directions

Prepare blackberry apricot topping by adding blackberries, apricots and water to a saucepan. Bring to a boil on medium high heat until slightly reduced. Remove from heat and add 1 teaspoon orange zest, vanilla and natural sweetener. Stir. Cover topping and set aside.

To make French toast, heat oil in a skillet over medium heat. In a pan mix eggs, egg whites and 1 teaspoon of orange zest to make the egg wash then coat each slice of bread with the egg wash. Cook each slice in the skillet for about 3 minutes per side or until golden.

Plate and top with blackberry apricot topping. Serve.

Pita Pocket Breakfast Sandwich

Ingredients

½ whole wheat pita pocket
½ cup baby spinach, chopped
2 grape tomatoes, halved
1 green onion, diced
1 large egg
1 large egg white
2 tablespoons Feta cheese crumbles
½ tablespoon milk
1 teaspoon olive oil
Salt, to taste
Pepper, to taste

Directions

Preheat oven to 350 degrees Fahrenheit. In a bowl whisk spinach, tomatoes, onions egg, egg whites, salt and pepper. Pour into skillet and place in oven for about 15 minutes or until eggs appear done. Sprinkle with feta and return to oven to melt cheese.

Brush pita with olive oil, wrap in foil and warm for 2 minutes. Remove eggs from oven, place in pita and serve.

Key Lime Protein Shake

Ingredients

Juice of 1 lime
½ avocado, peeled and pitted
½ cup plain Greek yogurt
½ cup almond milk
4 ice cubes
1 tablespoon natural sweetener
1 scoop protein powder
½ tablespoon vanilla extract

Directions

Blend all ingredients together and enjoy.

Whole Wheat Crepes

Ingredients

1 cup whole wheat flour

1 cup almond milk

¾ cup water

3 eggs

1 tablespoon honey

1 teaspoon pure vanilla extract

Pinch of salt

2 tablespoons plain Greek yogurt

Directions

Combine all ingredients into a blender. Pour batter into a non stick pan until it covers the pan. Immediately pull up the edges of the crepe with the spatula to make flipping easier. When the edges begin to bubble, check the crepe to ensure it is golden brown. Flip and cook other side until golden. Make second crepe.

Fill with fresh fruit and top with Greek yogurt and honey.

Fruity Breakfast Quinoa

Ingredients

¼ cup quinoa

¼ cup water

½ cup plain yogurt

¼ cup apricot nectar

½ apple, cored and diced

¼ cup blueberries

½ tablespoon almonds, chopped

Directions

Rinse quinoa and add to a pot along with water and apricot nectar. Bring to a boil. Reduce to a simmer and cover. Allow to cook for about 15 minutes or until liquid is absorbed. Remove from heat and allow to cool.

Once quinoa is cool, toss with apples, blueberries and almonds and finish with a dollop of yogurt.

Strawberry Banana Chia Pudding

Ingredients

¼ cup Chia seeds
1 tablespoon rolled oats
¾ cup almond milk, unsweetened
½ banana, sliced
⅛ cup strawberries, diced
½ scoop protein powder
½ teaspoon pure vanilla extract
½ teaspoon cinnamon
3 drops natural sweetener

Directions

In a bowl mix all ingredients except for fruit. Stir well to incorporate protein powder. Refrigerate for 10 minutes. Stir in strawberries and banana slices.

Amy Zulpa

Super Blueberry Smoothie

Ingredients

1 cup frozen blueberries

1 small banana

1 cup baby spinach

1 cup green tea, chilled

1 cup crushed ice

½ cup plain Greek yogurt

½ cup pomegranate juice, pure

Directions

Place blueberries, banana, spinach, tea, ice, yogurt and juice into a blender. Blend until smooth.

Spiced Pumpkin Protein Bars

Ingredients

½ cup canned pumpkin, organic

½ cup applesauce, unsweetened

1 cup whey protein powder

2 tablespoons pumpkin spice

½ cup honey, organic

1 cup peanut butter

1 ½ cup quick oats

Directions

Preheat oven to 350 degrees Fahrenheit. Roast oats on a baking sheet for about 15 minutes or until golden. Set aside and allow to cool.

Add remaining ingredients, including roasted oats, into a bowl and mix. Spread dough across baking sheet. Bake for 20 minutes or until golden brown.

Raspberry Watermelon Smoothie

Ingredients

2 cups frozen raspberries
1 cup diced watermelon
2 cups apple juice, unsweetened
1 tablespoon lime juice

Directions

Blend raspberries, watermelon, unsweetened apple juice and lime juice together until smooth.

Cheddar Chive Waffles with Pear Compote

Ingredients

1 cup quinoa flour
1 cup light spelt flour
1 3/4 cups milk
2 eggs
¼ cup safflower oil

4 teaspoons baking powder

¼ teaspoon salt

2 oz cheddar cheese, shredded

2 tablespoons chives, chopped

2 pears, peeled and cubed

½ cup water

Directions

In a saucepan add water and pears. Simmer on medium heat. Reduce heat and continue simmering for about 10 minutes or until pears have softened. Set aside to cool.

Preheat waffle iron. Begin making batter by combining milk, eggs and safflower oil. In a separate bowl combine dry ingredients which include quinoa flour, spelt flour, baking powder and salt. Mix wet and dry ingredients. Be sure not to over mix .Follow by folding cheese and chives into batter.

Pour about ⅓ cup of batter into each side of the waffle iron and cook until crispy. Repeat until all batter is used. To serve top with pear compote.

Chapter 6- 10 Clean Eating Soup & Salad Recipes

Artichoke Stem Soup

Ingredients

5 artichoke stems
¼ onion
2 cloves garlic
Low sodium stock
Olive oil
Sea salt
Pepper

Directions

Rinse artichoke stems under cold water. Thinly trim the rough outer edge from the artichoke stems.

Slice the stems into thin coins. Add 1 Tbsp olive oil to a medium saucepan. Add 1/4 chopped onion. Add 2 finely diced garlic cloves. Add pinch of salt and pinch of pepper. Cook until tender, about 10 minutes, stirring occasionally.

Add 2-3 cups low sodium stock to the pot. Remove from heat. Pour pan contents into a blender. Blend until creamy smooth. Pour soup into bowl.

Hearty Lentil Soup

Ingredients

1 cup uncooked lentils

1 sweet potato, chopped

1 zucchini, chopped

1 package fresh spinach

1 carton stock

1 package sliced mushrooms

2 cloves garlic

1 tablespoon Miso

1-2 tablespoons black sesame seeds or flax seeds

Directions

Pour 6 cups of broth into a medium pot. Add the lentils and sweet potatoes. Bring to a boil. Let cook about 15 minutes, until lentils are done.

Add vegetables to pot. Let cook an additional 15-20 minutes or until done.

Remove pot from stove and let it cool for a few minutes. Add the Miso. Using a ladle, spoon the soup into bowl. Top with sesame or flax seeds.

Nutmeg and Coconut Butternut Squash Soup

Ingredients

6 cups butternut squash

1 cups cold water
½ cup low fat coconut milk
1 tablespoon nutmeg
1teaspoon orange zest
Salt and pepper to taste

Directions

Add butternut squash to a 5 qt stock pot. Cover with water, until just covered. Bring to a boil. Reduce heat to low, cover with a lid and let simmer for 10 minutes or until squash is fork tender.

Turn off heat. Blend until velvety smooth. Add coconut milk, nutmeg, salt, pepper, and orange zest. Stir, until blended.

Spoon into a bowl. Drizzle with a bit of coconut milk and serve.

Avocado Black Bean Soup

Ingredients

2 cups cooked black beans
1½ cups stock
1 celery stalk, finely diced
1 heirloom tomato, chopped
2 garlic cloves, minced
½ red pepper, chopped
1 avocado, chopped
½ juice of a lemon
1 tablespoon cumin

Salt and pepper to taste

Directions

Add the celery, garlic, red pepper, and tomato to a pot. Heat until moist. Add the stock and let simmer about 5 minutes. Add 1 cup of the black beans to the pot. Stir. Let simmer about 5 minutes.

Pour contents into a blender. Pulse for 3-4 beats, then puree until smooth. Add the avocado, salt, pepper, and cumin. Pulse. Pour contents back into pot. Turn heat to low. Add the other cup of black beans. Stir. Add lemon juice. Stir.

Add bean soup to a bowl. Top with a dollop of Greek yogurt. Serve.

Ratatouille Vegetable Soup

Ingredients

1 teaspoon olive oil
5 cups chopped eggplant
1 pinch salt
1 onion
4 garlic cloves
1 red pepper
1 green pepper
5 cups acorn squash
⅓ cup broth
1 bunch fresh basil

1 fresh tarragon

Directions

Melt 1 tsp olive oil in the bottom of a 5 quart cooker pot on medium heat. Add the chopped eggplant. Add a pinch of salt. Let cook until brown and tender. Add a little water if needed. Remove the eggplant and set it aside.

Add 2 tsp olive oil. Add 1 chopped onion and 4-5 cloves of garlic. Cook until soft. Add the peppers. Cook until soft. Add the squash, tomatoes, and 1 1/2 cups stock. Add salt and pepper to taste. Stir. Cover with lid. Cook until veggies are soft.

Add 1 handful of fresh basil and tarragon, shredded. Stir. Spoon soup into bowl, and top with grated Parmesan cheese, if you'd like.

Spinach Berry Salad

Ingredients

1 8 ounce bag baby spinach
1 cup sliced raspberries
¼ cup Gorgonzola cheese
½ cup toasted pecans
Vinaigrette

Directions

Put spinach into a salad bowl. Top with sliced raspberries. Drizzle with vinaigrette. Top with pecans and Gorgonzola cheese. Serve.

Chunky Chicken Salad

Ingredients

Salt and pepper to taste
¼ walnuts
1 cup diced apple chunks, skin on
¼ cup purple grapes
½ cup plain Greek yogurt
2 tablespoons mayo
1 cup frozen peas, thawed
1 cup shredded chicken
1 cup diced celery
1 cup diced onion

Directions

Combine ingredients in a bowl. Serve.

Clean Eating Caprese Salad

Ingredients

3-4 Roma tomatoes, sliced
2 balls fresh mozzarella, sliced
1 handful fresh basil
Extra virgin olive oil

Salt and pepper to taste

Directions

Assemble tomato slices on a platter. Top with a slice of basil. Top with a slice of mozzarella cheese. Salt and pepper to taste. Drizzle with olive oil or balsamic vinegar and serve.

Clean Eating Brussels Sprouts Salad

Ingredients

2 cups shredded Brussels sprouts
Lemon juice from ½ a lemon
Olive oil
Salt and pepper to taste
Parmesan cheese
1 cup raisins

Directions

Place shredded sprouts into a salad bowl. In separate bowl whisk lemon juice and olive oil, until smooth. Drizzle over shredded sprouts. Add salt and pepper. Top with Parmesan cheese and raisins.

Clean Eating Broccoli Salad

Ingredients

2 crowns uncooked broccoli, cut into chunks

2 strips cooked bacon, cut into bits

½ red onion, chopped

⅓ cup slithered almonds

⅓ cup raisins

⅓ cup Greek yogurt (plain)

1 tablespoon red wine vinegar

2 tablespoon honey

Directions

Combine broccoli, bacon, almonds, onion, and raisins in a bowl. Toss well. In another bowl, mix yogurt, red wine vinegar with a fork, until smooth. Pour dressing over salad. Add salt and pepper. Mix well. Pour salad into a serving bowl.

Chapter 7- 10 Clean Eating Main Course Recipes

Barbecued Chicken Sunday Dinner

Ingredients

2 teaspoons mustard (prepared)
⅛ teaspoon pepper
4 pounds of chicken parts
⅓ cup onion (chopped)
3 tablespoons of butter
¾ cup of ketchup or tomato paste
⅓ cup vinegar
3 tablespoons of brown sugar
½ cup water
1 tablespoon Worcestershire sauce
¼ teaspoon salt
Cooking Oil

Directions

Heat oil in a large sauté pan; fry chicken until golden brown in color. Drain excess; position chicken into a 13 inch by 9 inch by 2 inch baking pan. Sauté onion in butter until onion becomes tender; add remaining ingredients. Simmer for 15 minutes. Spoon sauce over the chicken. Bake for 60 minutes at 350 degree Fahrenheit.

Dicey Porky Tenderloin

Ingredients

2 pounds of pork

3 tablespoons of chili powder

¼ teaspoon ground ginger

¼ teaspoon ground thyme

¼ teaspoon pepper

1 teaspoon salt

Directions

Mix seasonings well; rub over pork. Cover and chill 4 hours. Place onto hot grill and turn each side after 15 minutes or when the pork juices are clear or if the temperature of the pork is at 160 degrees Fahrenheit.

Chicken Cranberry Style

Ingredients

Cooked rice

Ground nutmeg

3½ cup all-purpose flour

¼ teaspoon pepper

6 boneless chicken breast cut into halves

¼ cup butter (softened)

1 cup cranberries

1 cup water

½ cup brown sugar

½ teaspoon salt

Directions

Mix flour, pepper and salt; rub onto chicken. In saucepan over medium heat brown the chicken with butter on both sides. Set aside. Add cranberries, water, brown sugar and a dash of nutmeg to saucepan. Stir for 5 minutes over heat. Add browned chicken. Cover and simmer 30 minutes.

Sausage Pie Delight

Ingredients

1 tablespoon Worcestershire sauce
2 tablespoons butter
½ chopped medium green pepper
½ chopped medium red pepper
1 tablespoon oil
3 cups cooked rice
5 medium size chopped tomatoes
4 ounces shredded cheese
1 teaspoon salt
2 tablespoons parsley (chopped)
1 teaspoon basil
1 cup bread crumbs
16 tiny pork link sausages
10 ounces corn

Directions

Put sausages into baking dish; bake in 350 degree Fahrenheit oven until light brown. Cut into pieces; place aside. In a sauté pan, sauté peppers in cooking oil for 5 minutes. Put into 2 quart casserole dish; add sausages and other ingredients over casserole. Bake without covering for 40 minutes.

Chicken & Rice Supreme Dinner

Ingredients

Chopped parsley
1 teaspoon poultry seasoning mix
1 fryer chicken (3 pounds), sectioned
⅓ cup all-purpose flour
2 tablespoons oil
1-½ cups uncooked rice
½ teaspoon salt
½ teaspoon pepper
1 cup milk
2-⅓ cups water
1 teaspoon salt

Directions

Coat chicken with flour. Sauté in oil over medium heat to brown chicken on all sides. Place rice, seasoning, milk and water into a greased 12 inch by 9 inch by 2 inch baking dish. Cover with chicken and top with foil. Bake in 350 degree Fahrenheit oven for 50 minutes. Garnish with parsley.

Garlic Pork Roast

Ingredients

1 teaspoon salt
¼ teaspoon cayenne pepper
½ medium green pepper
½ cup thinly sliced green onions
½ cup chopped celery
9 minced garlic cloves
1 pork loin roast approximately 5 pounds

Directions

Cut pockets into roast. Stuff inside pockets the pepper, onions, celery and garlic gloves. Season with herbs. Place into shallow baking pan. Bake at 325 degrees Fahrenheit for 3 hours.

Turkey Tetrazzini Peeni

Ingredients

1 jar pimientos
2 cups cubed turkey
1 cup shredded cheese
1 can mushroom soup
1 medium onion

⅛ teaspoon pepper

2 cans sliced mushrooms

⅓ cup milk

¼ cup chopped green pepper

¼ teaspoon salt

1 box of spaghetti

Directions

Cook spaghetti; drain. Place into large bowl; add other ingredients and mix. Transfer into greased 2 quart baking dish; cover with cheese and bake uncovered at 375 degrees Fahrenheit for 45 minutes.

Burger Town Burgers

Ingredients

6 strips of bacon

6 hamburger buns

1-½ pounds hamburger meat

3 tablespoons chopped onion

½ teaspoon pepper

1 cup shredded cheese

⅓ cup canned mushrooms

½ teaspoon garlic salt

¼ cup mayonnaise

Directions

Mix the hamburger meat, garlic salt, onion, pepper and salt into a mixing bowl. Form mix into six patty shapes. In separate bowl, mix mushrooms, cheese, mayonnaise and bacon; chill. Cook burgers over medium-high for 15 minutes, turning half-way through. Serve with shredded cheese.

Niberinia Rice Casserole

Ingredients

2 cups hot water
1 teaspoon cumin
1 package of instant rice
1 pound pork sausage
½ teaspoon garlic powder
2 medium chopped onions
2 beef flavored cubes
2 hot peppers, minced
2 medium chopped green peppers

Directions

Cook sausage in sauté pan with garlic and cumin powder while stirring often. Drain and add onions and peppers. Cook until tender. Place beef flavoring into hot water and add to sauté pan. Mix in peppers, rice and seasonings. Bring to boil then reduce to simmer. Continue uncovered for 10 minutes.

Broccoli Rice Casserole Supreme

Amy Zulpa

Ingredients

8 ounces cheese spread

3 cups cooked rice

1 small chopped onion

½ cup chopped celery

2 medium chopped onions

1 can mushroom soup

5 ounces evaporated milk

1 package chopped broccoli

Directions

Sauté the onions, broccoli and celery over medium heat in butter for 5 minutes and then add cheese and milk with mushroom soup. Place all items into greased 8 inch pan. Bake uncovered at 325 degrees Fahrenheit for 30 minutes.

ABOUT THE AUTHOR

Amy Zulpa writes on a myriad of topics but she always comes back to what she loves, food. She loves to eat and is always trying to find out what the healthiest trends are on the market so that she can try it out and see exactly how it works and how beneficial it is for those who try it.

Her latest focus is on eating clean in a bid to get those harmful toxins out of the body. Over time, the individual will feel that much healthier and also reduce the onset of numerous diseases.

www.ingramcontent.com/pod-product-compliance
Ingram Content Group UK Ltd.
Pitfield, Milton Keynes, MK11 3LW, UK
UKHW050419240426
12048UKWH00014B/710